Pirate Ships
&
Shakespeare's Lips

Poetry from the Ashes Reborn

By Janine Palmer (Silver Moon) CHT
A JP Silver Moon Series

Other books by Janine Palmer

MAIN BOOKS: (First Series)

Divine Heretic – Standing Holy
Divine Heretic – In Christ Consciousness
Divine Heretic – Sacred Scribe
Divine Heretic – Mystical Fire
Divine Heretic – Alchemist
Divine Heretic – Hierophant
Divine Heretic – Hidden Keys
Divine Heretic – Wordsmith
Divine Heretic – Song of the Seraphim
Divine Heretic – Anima Mundi
Divine Heretic – Echo of Thunder
Divine Heretic – Sword of Truth
Divine Heretic – Flaming Sword
Divine Heretic – Compassionate Non-Conformist
Divine Heretic – Sacred Smoke Signals
Divine Heretic – Arrows of Light
Divine Heretic – The Edge of Inner Truth

JP SILVER MOON SERIES: (Second Series)

Magic Quill, Sacred Sword
Fire & Thunder of the Bard
Mystical Whispers of the Soul
Mystical Whispers of the Scribe

Quicksilver Ink
Owl Feather, Sacred Scribe
Recalling the Mystery, Goddess of Arc
On Winged Destrier
Points of the Queen's Crown
Whispers of the Woods
Soul Speak, Mystical Heart
Extracting Wisdom from Experience
By the Light of the Silver Moon
Divine Illumination
Spiritual Alchemy
Lady of Fire
On Ravens' Wings
Enchanted Perspectives
Shields & Swords of Light
From Mystic Realms
Winged Revelation
Mystical Whispers of the Heart
Mystical Whispers of Wisdom
Cloaked Mystery & Swords of Truth
Sacred Temple
Twinkling of Twilight
Swords & Shields of Light
From Mystic Realms
Shadow Dance
Glimpses of Soul
Journal Entries from the Dragon Path
The Midnight Moon

From the Angels of Avalon
Once a Knight
Through the Mists & Shadows
Ink of Angelic Fire
Sacred Dialogue
Bardic Fire
Smoke Signals from Sacred Fire
Arrow Flights
Forged in Sacred Flame
Through Mystical Grace
A Priestess and a Poet Scribe
Poetic Ripples
Beautiful Reflections in Tarnished Mirrors
A Gypsy, a Knight, and a Philosopher
Mystical Journeys & Sacred Travelers
Mystical Muse
Pirate Ships & Shakespeare's Lips
Little Voices Carried on the Wind
Love Notes to Self
Pirate Ships & Shakespeare's Lips
Mystical Keys of the Soul
Oak Leaves & Acorns
Grails of Silver & Gold
Foxes & Flowers
Poet's Treasures
Bard's Treasures
Poetry from the Ashes Reborn
Glimpses of Mystical Prayers

Poetic Pinpoints of Light
Mystical Keys of the Soul
Divine Messages & Sacred Seeds
From the Ashes of Heretic Fire
Notes from Sacred Realms
Thoughts Infused with Love
A Cottage in the Heart
The Castle of the Heart
Whispers from Sacred Realms
From Bardic Wisdom Keepers

OWL FEATHER SERIES: (Third Series)

Gatekeepers of Sacred Temples
Remembering Forgotten Worthiness
Reflections of Perceptions
Weaving Beauty with Gratitude
This Book
Poetic Ministrations
Treasure Boxes & Tea Parties
Reflections of Worthiness
Mystical Ink
Perspectives, Paradigms & Possibilities
Gypsy Moon Boom
Mystical Chit Chat
Kingdoms Within

GENRE SPECIFIC BOOKS:
(Material Pulled from Main Books)

Energy Healing Wisdom
Spiritual Healing Wisdom
Divine Healing Wisdom
Rising Above Dogma
For Romance
Heart Speak
Romantic Reflections
Book of Worthiness
Apocalypse of Worthiness
Scriptures of Worthiness
Providence of Worthiness
Shamanic Energy Medicine
Sacred Shamanic Whispers
Shamanic Poetic Points of Light
Shamanic Healing Wisdom
Poetic Fire
Forged in Poetic Fire
Poetic Fire of the Soul

GENRE SPECIFIC BOOKS:
(Material pulled from the JP Silver Moon
Series and Owl Feather Series)

Sometimes, Always, Never
Sometimes, Then and Now

Souvenirs of the Soul
Bardic Passion Ignited
Poetic Flame Ignited
Forged in Poetic Flame
Pulse Point Poetry

Dedication

This book is dedicated to my family with deep love and to all the people who inspired me to write and to all poets and writers. The poetry contained herein is an acknowledgement to the healing powers of writing.

Writing about the importance of processing and releasing emotions becomes artistic expression. Energy needs to flow. These tales are about releasing those blocks. Trust the process of unfolding and spiritual evolvement.

Blessings, love and light.

Janine Palmer (Silver Moon) CHT

Acknowledgment of Gratitude

I am grateful for the blessings along my path, even the ones disguised as piles of shite. We learn from everything and everyone.

I am thankful for friends and guides and for so many amazing things learned and for the energy healing modalities I've learned, including and especially shamanic training, which helped to remember things, ancient things, I had forgotten.

I am thankful of emotional and spiritual healing which is an ongoing process. I am thankful for the opportunity to be of service and to help others when and if I can, when and if they ask for it.

I am thankful for such beautiful wisdom regained. I'm thankful for the inspiration for the writing and for how I am guided, known or unknown. I am thankful to be able to incorporate healing messages into the poems and messages.

I am thankful for what I've learned from spiritual teachers and biblical scholars and that I have always enjoyed reading which has opened me to so much knowledge and wisdom. I am grateful to all those who believed in me.

I want to say thank you to all the friends and family who have graciously supported me, taught me and redirected me. So many blessings – Blessings, love and light.

Janine Palmer (Silver Moon) CHT

Foreword

This little book reflects glimpses of experience and the wisdom gained from them. It reflects wounds, and the effects of the wounded who wound. It speaks of energy healing and forgiveness. It speaks of spiritual alchemy and the ascension of the spirit and the soul. It speaks of opening the door of the heart to love.

It speaks of battle scars and shedding skins and shells. It speaks of sacred temples and the fire of transformation. It speaks of rising above and moving beyond judgment, the spiraling, higher path to freedom through love and healing and releasing what does not serve. It speaks of the power of forgiveness. It speaks of things mystical and sacred. It speaks of magic.

It speaks of angels and dragons and divine love. It speaks of mirrors, treasures, keys and the mystical. It speaks of shadow and perspectives. It speaks of spirit, heart, soul and light. It speaks of deeper truth beyond belief and hidden keys. It basically shares the depth of love revealed by life experiences.

Introduction

What is shared in my writings often comes from wisdom gained through experiences, sometimes very grueling experiences. What is shared is also tools and knowledge gained from many healing modalities and certifications as well as much study of religions, religious scholars and spiritual teachers.

My work is for the purpose of reminding people to their worthiness and rising above judgement as far as condemnation of others due to lack of compassion or understanding.

These little stories offer information about healing self and stepping away from or letting go of toxic energies. Everyone interprets them differently. What I speak of comes from being shattered. Some of what I write comes from the parts of me which survived and endeavored to tell the tales and share what I learned.

I find myself called to be a voice for the abused and oppressed. Many of us do what we feel called to do for the collective, for the greater good…whatever our perception of that is.

There are many unhealed wounds in this world, in people, in the earth, and in animals. There are unhealed wounds in ancestral lines. These unattended wounds often cause people to go out and create more wounds.

We can do the work if we feel called to. The writing in this (and these) books are for those who have taken a step out on the path and are already moving out of stagnation and programming, or those who are ready to.

JP Silver Moon (CHT)

trŌoTH/
noun
1. 1.
the quality or state of being true. "He had to
accept the truth of her accusation."

synonyms: Veracity, truthfulness, verity,
sincerity, candor, honesty.

Source: Google

Truth is different for different people due to
their understanding of it, due to their
experiences, their 'beliefs', their conditioning.
Just because people understand things
differently doesn't make one version right and
the other version wrong. That's what your ego
wants you to think.

Your beliefs don't make you a better person
your behavior does. That is fact. I've seen
people of 'belief' who don't treat others 'well'.
They are acting according to their beliefs or
their interpretation of them. Their behavior,
somehow, does not reflect their belief. But
they think they know or are acting on 'truth'.
According to whom?

Contents

1 Sacred Temple 1

2 Glimpses of Soul 10

3 Mystical & Sacred 19

4 Divine Wisdom 28

5 Energy Healing 36

6 Fire of Transformation 47

7 Spiritual Alchemy 56

8 Worthiness & Wings 65

9 Blessed Be Our Magic 75

10 Deeper Truth 84

11 Mirror, Mirror 94

12 Battle Scars & Shedding Skins 104

13 Treasure & Keys 115

14 Suffering & Shadow 123

15 Whispers from the Heart 137

16 Light through the Cracks 146

17 Spoken from the Soul 155

18 Beyond Belief 163

19 Metaphoric Light 171

20 Perspectives 180

Sacred Temple

She walked a pathway through a Celtic
heritage,
And her energy drew you in,
She was an enigma and an inspiration,
The smoke from a fire shaman, floating on
the wind.

From castles and cottages of sacred places,
Of the sacred heart, the soul, and more,
A candle always burns from divine love,
Shining light through the keyhole of her
heart's ancient door.

She moves through the mists of memory,
Her angels are her illuminating guides,
She converses with Ascended Angels,
As she heals and raises her vibe.

She meditates with the vining flowers,
She communicates with the trees,
She works through the purity of the fire,
She listens to the voice of the breeze.

She has a sacred connection with the lake,
And her pen is sometimes her sword,

She's a spinner and weaver of many things,
But her favorite crafts are with her words.
She lives in the tower of a cottage,
Which looks like a castle, you know,
And her friends when they inspire her,
Help create the most curious glow.

Sacred Temple

There is a brotherhood.
There is a sisterhood.
They are one.
But many have forgotten.

What are you here to remember about who
you truly are which has nothing to do with
gender?
Gender is an experience to learn from.

We don't remember what we signed up for or
even what we write in dreams and waking
moments, but we live it through our choices.

Sacred Temple

She came equipped with dragon flame,
compassion, and a bucket of ice as an
antidote against the effects of hellfire.

She traveled with wolves and ravens, but
humanity didn't remember her.

Sacred Temple

He glowed in shades of bravery and
compassion which awakened sleeping
aspects of her dragon flame heart.

Sacred Temple

Her shield is her own love, trimmed with
wisdom.

Sacred Temple

All around us are stories. Some are touching, beautiful, and uplifting. Some are shocking, sad, or gruesome. The waves of vibrations and perspectives of life and the lenses we view it through.

Some people feel things very deeply and the suffering of the world often feels like too much to handle or process. Some days we might handle things better than others.

Sometimes we are able to feel the feelings and then shift out of them. We have empathy but we don't linger in sadness and grief. Sometimes a prayer might be all we can offer.

There are messages in stories, reminders. If we hear of someone doing something tragic because a person or a system lacked compassion when that person needed it the most, it might remind us to be aware to be more compassionate today.

Being of service to those in need might be the noblest of actions on this planet. Kindness is never wasted and the beauty of it ripples out continually from unexpected friends.

Sacred Temple

Sometimes there are elements to a story that
have different meaning to different people
and those people might focus, identify or be
triggered by something in ways others aren't.

Some people have experienced something
similar and may not have fully healed from it.
We might not be aware of it to any particular
degree when we share a story with someone.

We might not have intended any harm or
thought ahead to how something was going
to affect someone. We don't know until we
know. Sometimes we think we can openly
share things with people until we find out we
were wrong.

People are not on the same vibration
sometimes and those times might not be
known until they're communicated in some
way. Sometimes we learn we must hold
something back and tread carefully. We have
to be selective in what we share, more aware.

Sacred Temple

Glimpses of Soul

Some feel that gender neutrality might be about stepping out of roles, but from higher dimensions it might be about what is 'androgynous'.

It's about so much we've forgotten and about what we're remembering. We might not remember what we agreed to be to experience a particular life.

Many people work beautifully through certain roles or experiences. Others struggle. Some people don't feel at home, because we're not.

Some fight against programming. What we learn from any of it and all of it, is the wisdom we will carry forward with us.

Glimpses of Soul

Forest Poetry

She said, 'Cover me with a blanket,
Made from the forest ground,
Or the plaid passed down from our ancestors,
And weave me a flowery crown.

Let's fill a basket with gifts and treats,
For those in the forest who dwell,
Let's take with us our silver coins,
To toss in the wishing well.

Let's dance in the rain together,
Let's walk through the castle grounds,
Let's tell stories around the fire,
And discover what treasures are found.

Let's pick the thorns out of each other's
hearts,
Let's play hide and seek in the woods,
Let's listen to the birds and speak with them,
The way we always should.

Let's speak to the trees in prayerful ways,
Let's thank nature for her gifts,
Let's forgive everything that might hold us
back,
Thereby clearing our paths of rifts.

Let's read poetry out loud, new and old,
Let's decipher what it means,
Let's wade through the refreshing waters,
Of a purifying stream.

Let me hold you for as long as I want,
And breathe in your beautiful scent,
This would be something enjoyable,
As is any day with you spent.'

Glimpses of Soul

We often leave behind fragments of
memories which kindle the imagination
of others.

Glimpses of Soul

He didn't know if she was a tiger or a dragon
or a faerie queen. He was okay with all of it,
fascinating as it was to watch the changing
kaleidoscope of her energies.

Glimpses of Soul

Treasure gained through honesty is far more
valuable than what is gained through
dishonesty
or corruption.

How does it clothe the spirit and soul?

Glimpses of Soul

Fear is the farthest energy from Love. And
fear is often a liar.

Glimpses of Soul

There are times when people are honest with
themselves in ways they cannot communicate
to others who are not open to listen or hear.

Sometimes people are not willing to
acknowledge how their actions pushed
someone they love to a point to make a
decision they might find hurtful.

Glimpses of Soul

Mystical & Sacred

She lived in her own little world where she
traipsed through ancient forests collecting
rocks and bits of wood. She visited with the
shaman.

Her guardians were dragons and a griffin.
She had a fox for a pet. She lived in a cottage
and drew castles by candlelight.

Mystical & Sacred

She carried with her the energy of a lifetime
as a queen but also a witch, and a knight. She
was also told she had angel wings, but she
couldn't see them.

She was told she was the guardian of the
sword and poetry floated around her. She
captured it like butterflies and arranged it
bouquets on paper and shared it with
strangers.

Mystical & Sacred

She came alive in the rain. She made friends
with wolves. She spoke to ravens. Her heart
was a castle now surrounded by thorns.

She only found true peace deep in the forest
because her soul spoke the language of the
mountains. She was an earth spirit with
angel's wings.

Mystical & Sacred

He gathered the colors of poetry that dripped
from her pen and wove them into a tapestry
of feelings he wore like an invisible cloak to
infuse his heart and soul with the beauty of
her love.

Mystical & Sacred

What if what we believe is untrue and makes
us suffer.

What if it originates from fear?

Mystical & Sacred

Prayer from the heart and soul, not from
programming.

Mystical & Sacred

Prayer is beautiful. It's not only
communicating with higher creative source,
it's communicating with self.

Mystical & Sacred

Half Moon

She's the essence of rose petals on the
pathway,
She's the essence of fresh mint in her tea,
She's essence of the herbs in the garden,
She's the essence of love always free.

She's the essence of true compassion,
Ushered in with a welcome spring rain,
She's the essence of love being remembered,
As it flows from divinity, unrestrained.

She is the love of the feminine,
That honors the masculine here,
She is the sacred linen cloth,
Offered to dry your tears.

She is the words you long to say,
To yourself as you ascend,
She is the bridge you work to build,
And the salve for wounds to mend.

She is the mother and the sister,
She is the daughter and the wife,
She is the other half of the spark,
Of what we know or forgot is life.

Mystical & Sacred

Divine Wisdom

We teach what we need to learn as we are
learning it and we teach what we have
learned to the degree that we understand it.

Divine Wisdom

She knew the moment she met him that she
would marry him, and she did.

Divine Wisdom

He knew how to communicate with her soul.
It was the key to many rooms of
understanding. He spoke the language of her
love.

Divine Wisdom

What forces feed off the suffering of
mankind? Suffering that many religions
program us to believe and buy into.

Divine Wisdom

What true God would be so weak that it
would require blood sacrifice, war, and
suffering to sustain it?

Divine Wisdom

What if the source that created us was not a
vengeful, wrathful ideology of God?

Divine Wisdom

Dark forces seem to program the power of
the heart out of people who become like
drones.

Now it the perfect time to breathe life back
into our sacred hearts.

Divine Wisdom

Energy Healing

The energy of our truth reveals itself in
different ways. Paying attention to what we
feel helps guide us through doors we need to
go through.

Energy Healing

Peace might be something which whispers to us from our hearts…a place we simply step into. A place always waiting in our sacred energy fields. Something we bring with us wherever we go.

The key is not to allow the outside world to distract us from the beauty of it. Something we must not allow ourselves to forget. Peace is an aspect of our truth and a place where healing occurs.

Energy Healing

What was built before and passed down held
memories long forgotten which sometimes
appeared in dreams.

She listened as they spoke.

Energy Healing

We are connected to so many branches we're
not even aware of. But they continue to feed
us with information we call knowing and vast
amounts of love.

Energy Healing

Sometimes people perceive things incorrectly. There are instances where we don't remember something correctly. Things viewed through limited perspectives and then reacted to through the pain body.

We perceive it a certain way and that's the way we think it is. That's what we react to when we don't have full knowledge or truth and we don't know it, and then people suffer.

We should always be gathering information and it's important to remember that we gather more information through communication which we must then process.

We should continually be clearing debris from our energy fields and through processing and releasing in order to maintain the well-being of our energy body and sacred space.

Energy Healing

Some people are very aware that 'darkness', which is lower consciousness, works through religions and politics. Others are not aware.

People who are very ingrained in collective egoic group think are often battling something, but it might be the darkness in themselves and they're seeing it outside of themselves and then fighting people that aren't even their enemies.

Many are reacting to or through the programming. Inner battles, known or unknown. There is so much that is unknown, unseen, and misunderstood. What battles need to end today?

Energy Healing

She said, 'I want my messages to come from
as neutral a place as possible while still
shining light on that which is out of balance.'

Energy Healing

I'm thankful for those who
help us see ourselves for
who we really are.

Energy Healing

Sharing our stories can be helpful for us and for other people, especially when we speak about what we've learned from them.

There are times and reasons for us to share our stories. We might tell them many times. Then we might get to a point where when we tell them, we no longer have any attachment to them.

We don't feel triggered when telling them. We're just telling them to share the wisdom from them. It's an experience and we're not feeling harmed by them anymore. We're not feeling sad or bad about it.

We should tell our stories because there are people who will want to listen and who will get something helpful from it. This goes beyond holding onto a story because we get something out of continuing to struggle with it.

Energy Healing

Those who have the ability to help others to
heal sometimes lose their way like
everybody else. We all have certain gifts and
abilities we might be able to share, but we
still need to help ourselves from time to
time.

It's a process that's ongoing and sometimes
we don't see in ourselves what is needed.
I'm thankful for those who can help us focus
on areas where healing or love is needed.

Energy Healing

Fire of Transformation

Wisdom gained and applied began
to shine more light into and out of
her heart and soul.

Fire of Transformation

There are people who are like flames of transformation. They might kindle something in us. It might feel like they bring us back to life or reintroduce us to love again.

But like any earthly flame, when it runs out of fuel it burns down into a glowing ember and without something to feed it, grows cold and turns to ash.

That ash can add to the soil for future things to grow. We enjoy the warmth of seasons and experiences. We ourselves are spirits which are forged from sacred flame which is eternal.

Our experiences are for our souls to evolve. On earth we are in a realm of amnesia and free will choice. We are here to remember our divinity, with or without the help of other aspects of divinity's flame.

Fire of Transformation

He wondered how words could have the
power
to crack open the strongest armor for the pain
to escape its prion.

Fire of Transformation

Sometimes someone will be brave enough to
knock, and therein they shall discover
priceless treasure.

Fire of Transformation

What events in life have helped you to see
more clearly?

In what way has changing perspectives
liberated you from ignorance or darkness?

Fire of Transformation

He said, "Still chewing the bone, so to speak. The thing is, it's a bit ironic that you had a part in my awakened ability to handle opposing views again, without blowing my shit.

Coming out of the tent, so to speak...and trust me, this elephant in the room...this dichotomy between otherwise compatibility and joy...bothers me, and so I've been chewing the bone of contention.

Not angry, not ego, not mean or snarky. Also, not "dark", as your powerful text inferred, implying I have my head up the devil's ass or my own. And certainly not trying to change your view on anything...ok, stepping back again.

Detachment from the emotional...and searching for the root of the "bone". Harsh words are no help, hindering...no response is ok. Not really willing to have a valuable friendship go down...so again don't let us toss in the towel just yet."

She replied, "I don't think you're trying to change my view and what we know to be truth no one can change. If it causes angst, is it purely and wholly true? I've learned I don't have to defend or explain. It's not my job to convert anyone to anything. I'm on my own healing journey.

When someone casts insults and darkness and tar into my space, the only wise thing I can do is disengage. That behavior reveals something about the person who is triggered and responding in anger.

Do I like what's going on in the world? Of course not. Am I concerned for our children and grandchildren? Of course, I am. But I think they are wiser than we are, thankfully.

Too many people cling to and worship part of the whole, otherwise known as a side. The ego gets vicious in its role to protect what it doesn't recognize isn't complete or fully accurate.

We are only actors playing out a role on a shit-show stage. Things gets interesting when we start paying attention to the energies and thoughts and programming which drives us, or not.

From whence does it come and how does is serve our forward movement or hold us back? Is it helping us to heal?

Maybe instead of being unkind and being shitty to others, perhaps we could excavate our depths for stores of love as we cast out resentment, unforgiveness and our limited opinions or beliefs we mistakenly think are so holy when we don't even see how they cause us to treat others."

Fire of Transformation

Spiritual Alchemy

Some people have found they are far more
powerful without the shackles of hatred
trying
to drag them down into some false hell.

Spiritual Alchemy

Navigating this realm requires teamwork.

Spiritual Alchemy

Much of humanity needs an infusion of
remembering their divinity and worthiness
and a cleansing of the dark programming of
old energies.

Spiritual Alchemy

We might find that certain people hold keys
which unlock things in us. Spiritual
locksmiths who help us discover treasure
within.

Spiritual Alchemy

Sometimes we must retreat
from the wrath of the world.

Spiritual Alchemy

Wisdom comes from experience
and strength comes from knowing
when to let go.

Spiritual Alchemy

So many people don't know God because
they are in fear and too identified with ego or
the lower self.

Spiritual Alchemy

So many sleep and they don't know God.
They want power and control which is an
illusion.

Spiritual Alchemy

Worthiness & Wings

Sometimes we experience
our bravery in a dream.

Worthiness & Wings

She's like roses and coffee and
poetry wafting through his soul
on an autumn breeze.

Worthiness & Wings

We discover after going through certain shifts and initiations that we are not the same person. Nothing on earth including our energy is meant to be unchanging because it must move and flow. Evolving is the process of coming into fullness.

Worthiness & Wings

Mankind buys into the illusions of darkness
and thinks it needs to be rescued but only
needs to be rescued from the illusions and the
lies and the lower self.

Worthiness & Wings

There might come a time where we move
beyond belief and rise above religions.
Religions only point to God, they are not
God.

Worthiness & Wings

No particular religion is better than any other religion. (That is the trap).

Worthiness & Wings

Sometimes we are strong in ways we don't understand or can't explain. It's just a strength that's there when we need it. Other times we might need the strength another can offer us in a time of need.

Worthiness & Wings

Poetry is the language of love. But it's usually a much deeper degree or expression of love. Maybe some people haven't experienced that or they don't understand or remember.

It's not a language they currently speak or remember. Others are drawn to it and are nourished by it. It's code talk which awakens the soul. It takes us to other realms.

Worthiness & Wings

No one truly knows what anyone else really
suffers with. To judge or condemn without
full knowledge would be two things –
ignorant and unkind.

Worthiness & Wings

Blessed Be Our Magic

The language she spoke was poetry and
sometimes she used it to sharpen her sword.

Blessed Be Our Magic

He wore black as an unconscious symbol of his broken and dormant heart. He didn't want anyone to see in, so he closed the door. Curtains drawn, lights out.

But she could see into it anyway, she felt into it. She began to draw out the colors from it like threads and began to weave a tapestry of beauty from it to hold up to him to remind him who he is.

Blessed Be Our Magic

I'm thankful that my great, great grandmother left a journal of life growing up in Civil War times and what life was like living on acres and acres of farmland. The loneliness and the beauty.

I was able to get to know her through her writing in ways I wouldn't have if she hadn't left a written record. She wrote incredibly beautiful poems. Inspiration.

I encourage people to write stories to be passed down to future generations.

Blessed Be Our Magic

She shines in colors he can feel and taste.

Blessed Be Our Magic

Beware of impostors of illusion.

Blessed Be Our Magic

She said, 'For me it will always be about
love.'

Blessed Be Our Magic

The magic is the connection between two people, recognized, celebrated, and honored.

Blessed Be Our Magic

We are all expressions of Creative Source at different levels of awakening and awareness.

Blessed Be Our Magic

Deeper Truth

Illusion often creates monsters that don't really need to be battled or slayed when wisdom is a sharp blade that cuts through smoke screens and puppet strings.

Deeper Truth

Sometimes something resonates. You feel the truth in it. You know the truth in it. It goes beyond belief or simply believing in it, and it doesn't function through fear or unworthiness programming.

Deeper Truth

I'd like to share my limited perspective about something that also seems to be a limited perspective.

While there is truth in what I'm about to comment on, I feel there is more truth than what was stated and I'm sharing it here for reflection in case it might be of interest.

There was a post on social media that some girls don't want to be like 'Bond' girls. Some are more about wolves and feathers in their hair, etc. Free spirits. More individual and not fitting into any particular mold.

Someone made a comment to the effect that women who lack faith in their femininity and their 'ability to attract and keep a strong man' cultivate masculine qualities to compensate.

To which my reply or response would be: Some women might not choose to 'attract and keep a man' because they are balanced in their own masculinity because they have been that before and they carry it with them. Some people stay together out of mutual respect and the attraction of souls.

The person went on to state that a woman preferring to be masculine to feminine will struggle to fulfil her innate need to build and maintain a family, via bloodline or in a social setting.

He also said that femininity plays an important role in community, collective and mental health and that its folly to encourage girls to deny their femininity to strive to be masculine, powerful and strong, as if femininity isn't already that in its own way or that a woman or anyone else needs to fit into any role.

There are women who are strong or balanced in their masculinity (and their femininity) who, without trying, draw many men to them. There are women who have been married to men for decades which might not have as much to do with their 'femininity' as it does with the beauty of their souls. If the feminine is strong and balanced as well, it is a win, win. Balance is always a win.

I don't know many people who encourage
women to be masculine. Some women are
tomboys. So what? Most of them were not
taught to be that way.
Perhaps some women have had to become
strong or stronger in their masculinity (or
their femininity) in order correct the
imbalance of the patriarchy. Some fake,
overzealous, self-proclaimed, superiority
complex which has squashed the feminine
into boxes and roles. Not anymore.

It might just be part of the recalibration of the
feminine to where it should rightfully be. If a
woman is more feminine, that is probably her
choice or what is emanating from her soul,
not because she has to play a role to please
any man. That would be fake or possibly
manipulative.

The feminine expresses itself in many ways
and is always beautiful and should always be
celebrated and protected. Of course it's
needed in societies and families and
communities all around the world. It always
has been. Some people honor it more than
others.

The strength of the feminine is determined by
the lifetimes she or he has led and the
wisdom that soul brings forth into other
lifetimes, even within a single lifetime. A
man might be drawn to the feminine for
different reasons.

Some admire her strength and for some men
she is too strong and too powerful, whether
she's wearing a sundress, lingerie, jeans, or
armor.

She is there to do what she signed up for
through how her soul is called and not simply
to please the ideologies of those in masculine
form.

Deeper Truth

Man disrespecting woman, is dangerous to
man.

Deeper Truth

Darkness feeds off negativity, fear, anger,
guilt, shame and unforgiveness.

Deeper Truth

Some say or think they are doing God's work
but sometimes their God is a devious
impostor and they know it not.

Deeper Truth

Mirror, Mirror

Sanctuary can be many places where peace
and creativity dwell. We might even bring it
with us where we go.

Mirror, Mirror

Some people are noticing that there are those who say or complain that another 'side' is doing exactly what their 'side; is doing, but they don't see it.

Many don't see the corruption of the sides they cling to and defend.

And the drama continues where lack of knowledge creates suffering.

Mirror, Mirror

She said, "Some people seem to revere the hatred they cling to which keeps their hearts closed off to discovering certain truths which could life them out of despair.

The hatred which closes hearts and minds for protection or creates places for dark things to feed.

For truth to be able to enter, more knowledge is needed and for that there must be open doors for it to flow through."

Mirror, Mirror

Many people speak and write about the same or similar things, all over the world, who don't know each other or what the other is doing, until they meet and maybe they never meet.

People are guided by something higher than their earthly personality. Some people come across the same teachers or books and learn similar things which they begin to apply to their lives and teachings.

Many people are inspired by poets, song writers and spiritual teachers. They absorb what they learn and soon they are speaking the same language to others. Many people are writers because it's part of their soul. What matters is the message and the energy in which it's delivered.

Sometimes things are taken and used in ways which aren't quite ethical, and which don't honor the person who created it. There are those who pretend something is theirs and take credit for it when it's not theirs.

Similarly, there are those who mistakenly
believe someone took something from them
when it isn't true.
There is no proof, only misperception which
misleads and creates suffering. Too many
people are accused of doing things they did
not do.

There are those who haven't taken anything
from anyone, but because it's of a similar
subject, or language, or wording, others
might think it was stolen, when in fact it
might just be the same frequency working
through them, which is love.

Mirror, Mirror

Sometimes people read something deep and meaningful, poetic or otherwise, which they will reflect on and get something powerful from.

Depending on where someone is on their healing journey and what kind of communicator they are, they may or may not speak up about what they feel about what they read.

Some people are not afraid to openly share how something made them feel. Others are not comfortable doing so. Some people are successful communicators, others are not. Some people are outgoing. Some people are shy.

When a writer or a poet shares a message on a public platform, many of them do so from a place of love. They are sharing something they survived or learned from without knowing who it might speak to or in what way.

Poetry and stories shared are often gifts
which writers share for healing and
upliftment. When people communicate that
something was helpful, it inspires the writer
to keep doing the work. Many writers are
brave to share what they share.
If something is helpful to another person,
that's what matters the most. Sometimes
people share something with others they find
to be beautiful and helpful, so that act of
bravery in sharing might have a very
profound ripple effect the writer might not
even be aware of.

Not everyone is adept at expressing what
they feel or how they might be struggling
with something. Just because they don't
express their feelings about it doesn't mean
it's not appreciated.

Thank you to all the writers who share
beautiful messages with the world, for your
bravery and for putting the language of your
heart into a tapestry of words which some
people need to read, hear and feel.

Mirror, Mirror

Some people become aware that darkness uses religions and ideologies for nefarious purposes.

Mirror, Mirror

There are times we just don't feel at home,
even in our own homes or around our
families. Life is always changing around us
and within the lives we create.

We are affected by what's happening to
others which shifts and changes our energies
and perspectives.

We might feel unsettled or like we don't
belong somehow. It's probably an indicator
of change or that something needs to change,
even if it's our perspective about something.

Time alone for reflection and time in nature
can be very helpful and healing to gain a
deeper perspective or even to let go of
something to make room for what we want to
invite into our lives.

Home is what you make it, and home is what
you bring with you wherever you go. Home
is the beauty to bring to a place.

Mirror, Mirror

Battle Scars & Shedding Skins

Some people don't like being screwed by the
system. Others seem to adjust to it and
tolerate it quite well.

But not those who are suffering due to it, and
there are many.

Small steps in the energy of truth make big
changes where they are desperately needed.

Battle Scars & Shedding Skins

She said, 'I'm sorry if I refrained from
demonstrating love when I was recovering
from the starvation of not receiving it in
certain ways.'

Battle Scars & Shedding Skins

He said, "It's sad when people target you."

She said, "But its great inspiration for dialogue to go more deeply into different perspectives on different subjects. Misunderstandings lead to reactions we wouldn't expect. What do we learn from it?"

Battle Scars & Shedding Skins

There are different types of non-conformists
breaking free of dark shackles, which might
be perceived as enemies through the energies
of ignorance and fear, as history continues to
reveal.

Battle Scars & Shedding Skins

There are those who might make you face
your hatred or unforgiveness in order to cut it
loose, who are temporarily perceived as 'the
enemy'… when what they really are is a soul
messenger trying to remind you of the light
in your heart.

Battle Scars & Shedding Skins

There are people who are deeply programmed through their culture or religion, that are against things they don't understand.

This is due at least in part to their programming which limits, filters, clouds, or otherwise obscures their view of a much bigger picture.

These might be stumbling blocks on your path which you will learn how to move around or climb over.

You might even discover your wings which will help you elevate above things of a lower vibration which would try to hold you back through the energy of fear and the lie of unworthiness.

Your worthiness is the love of God which lives in you.

Battle Scars & Shedding Skins

Sometimes people hold onto hurt which is false. People often react to what they perceive, but don't realize that what they perceive is not an accurate or full truth. They are missing information.

If they were in possession or awareness of further information, they likely wouldn't feel so hurt and carry the unnecessary burden of pain created by misperception and misunderstanding.

Battle Scars & Shedding Skins

There are those groups mistreat women due
to fear and overinflated egos, and there are
those who are rising above and moving out of
that false power.

Battle Scars & Shedding Skins

After discussing certain behaviors of humanity my friend said, "Is this who we are? Is this who we're becoming?"

These are the choices we must make. These choices are about vibration.

Battle Scars & Shedding Skins

On the other side of letting
go is freedom. Freedom to
choose something else.

Battle Scars & Shedding Skins

Treasure & Keys

There are many who are
holding swords, laying
them down, or guarding
them.

Treasure & Keys

We come to know and share
compassion in our own divine
ways.

Treasure & Keys

She was a treasure box
waiting to be opened by
love.

Treasure & Keys

Like-minded people don't always understand things the same way and might not be functioning in the same vibration or dimension, which is consciousness.

Many are conscious of things others are not conscious of. Everyone is walking their own path of awakening, becoming and healing or not knowing how to heal.

There is so much suffering which has been passed down through the generations, including dark programming from old energies which cannot and will not be sustained in the higher levels of consciousness which earth and humanity are moving into.

We must learn to heal it, to stop keeping the suffering alive through loops of stagnant hatred which doesn't help us or our ancestors. It must stop somewhere. Are we the warriors for that job? Have we learned to harness the power of forgiveness?

But we must get there through choice. There are those who will choose the old paradigm of suffering and you might have to leave them where they are.
What is reflected or created by how we see other people and how we treat them and how we see or don't see ourselves?

This also relates to the treatment of animals and anything of the earth which should be honored and cared for.

Treasure & Keys

Meet them in their heart space and know
their beauty.

Treasure & Keys

Life sometimes requires us to muster strength
we didn't know we had.

Treasure & Keys

Suffering & Shadow

Sometimes we make friends that are so dark
we have to leave them in the shadows they're
not ready to come out of, and they might try
to make it our fault. And when we call them
out on it, they might chuckle wickedly as we
cut the cord.

Suffering & Shadow

Sometimes people might call you arrogant
when they can't handle the power of your
flame.

Keep being humble and compassionate, even
when you are misunderstood.

If you're watching for rabbit holes, you can
step over them.

Suffering & Shadow

There are those who seem to thrive on
judging others in order to feel superior.

Their egos are hungry.

Souls might be hungry too, but they are fed
with love.

Suffering & Shadow

There are those who are going to choose anger, hatred and rage, and we might have to choose to walk away and just vibrate higher.

Suffering & Shadow

Some people lean heavily toward in certain directions or toward certain parties. Some are 'extreme' which often reveals a need for healing or balance.

They seem to function from a pack mentality, and they want to fight against something or someone. If you point out or reflect their hatred back to them, they will likely perceive you as 'the enemy'. They might shun you. Low vibe as hell.

They declare a personal war which enhances their suffering, even if they are not aware of it. Unfortunately, there are those who feed off hatred.
However, some people walk away from negativity to protect their energy which is not shunning it's disengaging.

Some people who detach are not doing it because they are judging someone to be 'beneath' them, they just choose not to be around a vibration that doesn't resonate. Others can often see things about us we don't see in ourselves.

There are those who don't judge people, they continue to hold space for those they love and are completely open to the communication that would be required to resolve a situation and reestablish a friendship, but it takes two.

There are those who aren't willing to do the work and self-reflection and letting go that would be required to heal something they judge or perceive to be another's fault.

Sometimes we misunderstand another, or they misunderstand us, which creates so much unnecessary suffering which honest communication could remedy.

Then there are those who discover they've been mired in certain 'programming', and they learn to break free. They step out of the box. There are those who free themselves from certain things, including controlling belief systems which function through fear in order to control. The fear mongering in this world is off the charts. Two words, 'Don't Engage'.

Many of those people who are standing in their truth are not recognized or honored by those who are still controlled by the system, or their fear, or their insecurities, or the false programming of unworthiness they have adopted and cling to unconsciously.

They embrace the battles which keep ignorance alive and in control. Many are unknowingly mired in ego battles and the sludge they create, flinging tar at each other instead of climbing out of the pit.

Some people don't see the box they are in. They're being led around by the ego where they judge others as wrong in order to make themselves feel right.

They will do things which are not wise or healthy because they caught up in group mentality and the matrix wars. Defending it gives them purpose, even if that purpose is functioning in ignorance or feeding the monsters created by ignorance unconsciously.

When we no longer feel the need to fight other people due to differing viewpoints, we are vibrating in higher dimensions.

When politics or religions don't trigger us to be haters, we are vibrating higher. When we recognize the extreme negativity of 'the news' and how we are being programmed and we choose to disengage, we are vibrating higher.
Many people are not seeing higher truth because they are still seeing and feeling the need to defend the programs which are the illusion.

There are many who function like this because they are unhealed. Many people are not open to considering other perspectives or viewpoints, yet sometimes that is the only way to begin to break free of the stagnant loops they are stuck in.

Sometimes we must climb to higher ground to get a better view of what the actual hell is really going on in the drama stage battle zones of earth school. And hopefully we don't step on or disrespect others who are

trying to the same thing. We rise together but
it must happen through choice.

Sometimes we must forgive in order to rise
and that especially includes forgiving
ourselves. It means making peace with things
and people. It will probably need to involve
some type of communication, even if it's
only through prayer.

It will probably involve not hating on anyone
for things we perceive to be wrong when we
don't have all the information or the facts,
especially if we're not open enough to listen
to or hear another person's viewpoint or side
of the story.
Sides are only perspectives. They are limited
perspectives. But the ego hates to be wrong
or to be perceived as 'wrong' when we all
live in a realm of incompleteness where we
have forgotten our divinity.

It requires being honest with ourselves and
being kind to others. Not just certain people
we perceive to be 'worthy', who are part of
our club. Beware of clubs of ignorance which
are collective egoic groups too identified
with thoughts, beliefs and ideologies.

We might have to remove the energy of 'holier-than-thou' banner we've unknowingly been wearing, in order to actually begin to truly discover God and love in ourselves and others.

What many people worship might not be of the highest frequency, and they might not be aware of it. Many people do not see the effects of their behaviors because they feel justified in them.

We might need to let go of a lot of things, including ideologies, beliefs and programming to get back to the love of who we truly are. There are those we might have cast aside who miss us because true 'us' has been lost, buried, or hijacked by shadowy systems we don't yet recognize as such. The road back to self can be a lonely road at times where we must learn to stand in the power of our light, even when others cast shadows or stones.

When others falsely judge us through their ignorance or tainted lenses, we must cleanse that dirty or low vibrational energy from our sacred space.

When we disengage from the matrix and
come back to truth, we become a brilliant
beacon of light and people will be drawn to
that light.

Suffering & Shadow

There are those enmeshed or entangled in certain groups or sides. Maybe it's extremism, maybe it's not. It's group think. It's programming.

It might be connected to an unhealed part of them, and something triggers them, so they may feel they have something to fight against and something to pour their hatred into.

There are many unknowns. Many people are drinking the 'kool-aid', absorbing poisons. Knowingly or unknowing taking into their bodies and their energy fields, things which are toxic.

They're going to do what they're damn well told and they're going to fight for it, even if it's wrong, even if they are in ignorance and don't know it.

We are all watching something terrible and something amazing unfold and play out before us in the external. What about the internal?

Something collective is revealing itself that
we must decide how to respond to on an
individual level.
Things are often not what they seem. There is
darkness behind the curtain. Some can see it,
sense it, and feel it…others cannot.

There are those who want to 'rule the world'.
There are ways we might engage or
disengage, through choice and perspective.

We all have limited perspectives and do the
best we can through whatever programming
does or does not control us.

Suffering & Shadow

Whispers from the Heart

In a cottage in the frozen woods, an ice king
lit a candle for a free-spirited girl who didn't
know she would soon be queen.

Whispers from the Heart

Sometimes pictures can say what words can't
and sometimes the intensity of a glance
speaks what neither words nor pictures can
ever say. It's something you feel and see. The
language of energy.

Whispers from the Heart

Sometimes carefully selected words we read reach right into our hearts and speak the words we didn't know how to say. They speak to and from our hearts in a wave of relief through the expression of understanding.

Whispers from the Heart

He said, 'My heart roars.'

She said, 'Good'.

Whispers from the Heart

There are those who want to allow themselves to be loved, truly loved, but they have forgotten how due to trauma. The effects of deep trauma and unconscious trauma responses.

Whispers from the Heart

There are times we must let something go
with love we will not truly lose. It's time for
it to transcend a certain experience and take
another form.

Whispers from the Heart

So many teachers have come and gone who
shared goodness and light with the world that
was unrecognized by the masses due to
limited perception and rigid belief systems
fueled by fear.

But fortunately, there were seeds of truth that
took root and are still growing and
blossoming far and wide, deep and tall.

Whispers from the Heart

We all have to take turns with certain things.
When we learn patience, acceptance and
forgiveness we become a different kind of
powerful. When we are motived by love
rather than being manipulated by fear, we
function from a different kind of strength.

Whispers from the Heart

Light through the Cracks

Labels limit understanding. We never have full knowledge of anyone or anything.

Light through the Cracks

What is happening in our country (and world) today some would say is a total shit show. It's fake as fuck. Some people can see it, others cannot. It is a time of apocalypse, to reveal what was hidden.

There is that which is inauthentic which must hide and steal because it is weak. Stealing innocence through the corruption of ignorance that it is. In one word, diabolical.

But also, amongst the chaos is 'good'. There are good people all over the world. People who are kind and compassionate.

Those who would help rather than harm. Those who are doing good words. The healers and the peacemakers. The messengers and those who work to restore balance. The protectors and guardians.

We must decide who we are and what we're called to do. We evolve through the process of alchemy. There are those we care about who might take a longer road to get there because they have more to learn.

Light through the Cracks

To hate anyone or anything reveals
something that needs to be healed in self.
Where do the roots go? What is the wound?
What is the trigger?

Shadow work is discovering what is
unconscious in us. It's about becoming
aware, letting go, making peace, forgiving
and healing.

Light through the Cracks

If only we could all learn not to be drawn
into the division. If only we could part the
mists, find the good, and celebrate it in each
other.

Light through the Cracks

She said out loud to something on her computer screen on a social media site, "Stop sucking in all the drama and vomiting it back out again. You're just creating more drama infused with horrendous negativity, confusion and chaos."

And then she laughed.

Light through the Cracks

People will judge. People will be jealous.
People will shun. So often it's a reflection of
them, not you. These behaviors reflect what
needs healing.

Light through the Cracks

Be you. Be yourself. Sometimes people
aren't ready for who you are. That's okay. Be
you anyway.

Light through the Cracks

She said, "After some deep study, it became
apparent that some extremists seem to
confuse
the devil for their god."

Light through the Cracks

Spoken from the Soul

Chariots

A familiar quill from ancient days,
Or a sword come hither to part the haze,
The mists of time or illusion's grave scene,
A captain returning to navigate the dream.

A crown invisible and a love that is not,
The trouble which arises from what we
forgot,
As the mystery opens a fraction at a time,
For those paying attention there is treasure
sublime.

Chariots of fire through dimensional force,
Incinerating the remnants of darkest remorse,
Forgiveness a light ship, from God's temple
room,
Holy, holy, holy shining light through the
gloom.

Words all around us, puzzles disorganized,
While truth whispers to us, from beyond all
false disguise,
Fields of duality from a dark matrix, hell
bent,
Where stepping out of ignorance, is a
gauntlet intense.

The soul in amnesia, the logical mind,
The spirit, the treasure, some can't seem to
find,
The emotional body, a difficult test,
And the truth of inner knowing, where grace
always rests.

Janine Palmer (Silver Moon)

Spoken from the Soul

In Poetry

He spoke to her in poetry,
Because it was one of the keys to her heart,
He entered the space with flaming torch,
To light places closed or dark.

He entered with a humble respect,
He entered thankfully through grace,
He entered a sacred sanctuary,
A brilliant and glowing place.

He left a gift of love there,
A gift that made her smile,
A gift he'd given her many times before,
A treasure which wouldn't beguile.

The truth of love purely given,
Expecting nothing in return,
But return his love she always did,
Through what balance surely earns.

He spoke to her in silence,
He spoke to her in a glance,
He spoke to her without words,
And what they felt was more enhanced.

In her heart were felt the truer things,
Which are obscured on the face of the earth,
And when that energy flowed through them,
It was a type of soul rebirth.

Janine Palmer (Silver Moon)

Spoken from the Soul

Periodically people will arrive who speak the
language of your soul, whereby you can
engage
and delight in conversations of deeper
divinity
with kindred spirits.

Spoken from the Soul

Perhaps a deeper look into the term 'belief'
might reveal it to be limited and limiting.
Perhaps our journeys are meant to lead us
back to knowing, our own truth, which we
forget when we come here.

Spoken from the Soul

Thoughts can create misery. They can also inspire us. They can propel us forward or hold us back. They might help us to filter the perspectives and experiences of life.

Thoughts test us. They might feed programs. Many thoughts that filter into our awareness are not true, but if we believe them to be true, we might suffer because of it. Let thoughts flow and not get stuck.

Spoken from the Soul

Beyond Belief

Belief is powerful, whether true or false. It can be used to propel you forward or hold you back. Truth is stronger, more powerful, more pure.

If you listen quietly truth will speak loudly from the kingdom within. If you clear away limiting programming, it will reveal hidden doors to forgotten treasures.

Beyond Belief

It can be shocking how angry some people
get when their mask slips and they are seen
for who or what they truly are.

It can be destructive when people try to
blame someone else for what they project or
won't take responsibility for.

Some people create stories or believe gossip
about others and treat them terribly due to
lies.

Some people tell lies about others, and they
somehow seem to believe them and use them
as a target for their hatred.

Many people have experienced this or
watched it play out.

These dramatic spectacles teach us a lot
about vibration and when we should move
away from energies or behaviors which don't
resonate.

People who are suffering often reveal it
through unconscious behavior patterns, but
you don't need to be a target for their poison
arrows.

Beyond Belief

Some people are so ingrained in their
obedience
to the limitation of what they 'believe'.

They don't seem comfortable learning about
what they don't know, and they're
programmed to fear what they don't
understand.

Beyond Belief

Sometimes people need to 'pick a side', something that resonates with their awareness or unhealed traumas for a time. That limited perspective and how it appears due to the information we possess or lack, known or unknown.

There might come a time when the penny drops and we choose not to be on a side because we recognize the imbalance, because we realize each side has 'issues', because we are gathering more information and because we now chose to be on a path of seeking knowledge.

Some people are not open to learning what they don't know and so they cling to a side and defend it which often bolsters the ego. Other people start to see that things are not what they thought they were, and their perspectives begin to change. This is why it is said that knowledge is power.

Some people disengage from sides and walk what is called the middle path because they are gathering information from all sides and

applying it in ways that resonate with their
soul. Beyond logic and limitation because
they are working through their heart.
There are groups and entities, for millennia
and ongoing, which withhold knowledge
from the masses in order to manipulate them.
Some are aware of this, some are not.

It's very powerful when a person realizes
they don't have to make someone else wrong
to bolster a belief which is incomplete. We
all exist in a realm or cloud of unknowing.
Truth is within from whence intuition speaks.

Initiates are seekers of knowledge, applying
wisdom to pave their pathway out of shadow
lands.

Beyond Belief

There's a difference between having
confidence in your truth and arrogance, and it
may or may not be the difference between
ego or higher self.

Beyond Belief

She said, 'I know many people who see the
world through a particular lens, who have
concerns and want to heal something, and I
endeavor to be that voice sometimes. I can
only write about what it means to me or how
I understand it, and I'm still learning.

Beyond Belief

Metaphoric Light

Sides or the illusion of them is often the
enemy, that and perspectives,
misunderstandings, and a whole lot of ego.

Metaphoric Light

We all have things to work through and learn
from. Our minds and the programs they run,
play tricks on us.

The heart holds the wisdom we seek.

Metaphoric Light

He said, "Who really knows the truth?

She replied, "No one. We are all missing information. The soul knows. The spirit knows. The sacred heart knows. The Akash knows.

But many humans aren't in touch enough to rediscover certain truths because the mind, the ego and programming get in the way.

There are truths beyond 'logic' we must ascend to higher dimensions to discover."

Metaphoric Light

Understanding comes and goes,
Sometimes with thorns like any rose.

Metaphoric Light

In previous days and centuries, many people were tortured, traumatized, abused, and killed due to misunderstanding. Due to believing things that were not true and acting out of fear.

Today it seems the opposite is occurring. There are those who are known to be perpetrators of certain lewd and unconscionable actions against people, yet they are not being brought to task or to justice for their crimes against humanity, innocent beings, and children, as well as political crimes and media corporations pave the way for and cover up their dirty deeds.

It's time to take a closer look at what's going on in our world, stand strong against cruelty, and speak up and take action toward or against what is bringing the vibration of this world down or keeping it down, and what needs to be changed and healed, individually and collectively.

Metaphorical Light

What branches do we choose to climb or
extend as we move through ideologies on our
way back to truth?

Metaphoric Light

Revelation comes in many colors of understanding and misunderstanding.

How does it translate within?

Metaphoric Light

How brave to live differently in a world that
doesn't recognize your beauty because it has
forgotten it's own beauty and then judges you
through the lens of what it's lacking.

Metaphoric Light

Perspectives

How can we stand separate from hatred if we exist in it? We can recognize it for what it is and choose not to engage in it. We can choose not to be drawn into it, even in the process of working to change it.

There is separation which is designed to keep people fighting against each other for dark things to feed on and manipulate. It might help to understand it in the way of vibration.

People vibrate at higher or lower vibrations which might change with experiences through grueling initiations and through evolution, healing and choice. Some people have experienced terrible or beautiful things which others have not, so perspectives are not the same.

People might not like the hatred they see oozing out of people all around them, but they don't 'hate' those people for being in that vibration or they would also be functioning from that lower vibration.

We can disengage and detach, which is a type of 'separation'. A choice from and for a different vibration. Not a type of separation

which controls people from exterior sources
or entities through programming, anger, or
fear.
There are those who use people's unhealed
wounds to trigger them to fight amongst each
other.

It's happening all around us. Some people are
looking at others and finding fault, they
aren't looking within. There is power in
being in charge of our own reactions and
becoming aware from whence they come.

Perspectives

How long does a person copy someone else's
style before they create or get in touch with
their own?

Perspectives

Hate might be a lower vibration or a lower consciousness. It might reflect a wound being projected out onto another who triggers us.

We should not have to accept what we hate but we might need to heal that hate in order to rise above it or out of it. The hatred is a symptom of something deeper in the individual or the collective.

Perspectives

No one should have to embrace enemies of freedom. Hatred comes from fear. Hatred is destructive. Hatred separates us from love.

People are afraid of what they don't understand and of what goes against cultural and religious programming.

Everyone here is free, or is supposed to have free will to do and be what they choose, even against opposition. This is how we learn.

Many people judge or hate others due to disagreement or misunderstanding. It might be terribly imbalanced or unfair to hate someone for choices which are different than ours, especially if you haven't lived the traumas they have.

People react from what is unhealed in themselves or their family lines, even if they are not aware of it.

Division interferes with ascension out of the hellish places or energies on this planet which were hijacked by ignorance.

Perspectives

There are those who hate whatever current administration is in 'power', which is attempting to function through whatever agendas control it behind the scenes, however real or fake they are.

Are they wrong?

There are those who are trying to walk the middle path and not lean too far into any realm of extremism.

Are they wrong?

There are those who are healing, those who are trying to heal, and those who don't recognize that healing is needed.

Are they wrong?

There are those who have degrees of awareness about how to go about healing and try to help by sharing it.

Are they wrong?

Just because people try to do what they feel is right doesn't make them 'Enlightened Ones',

but it might make them targets for the ire of
those who are angry.

There are those who are very wounded,
resentful and angry who are easily
manipulated by forces who purposefully
trigger those wounds. And those who are
being manipulated through their unhealed
issues are typically not aware that they are
being played like pawns on a chessboard.

Perspectives

Why is it that certain people on certain 'sides' become haters of those on perceived other 'sides', and then target or ostracize them, even when they haven't ever talked about important life issues?

There are always things we don't know about people or situations, but when we find out, it changes our perspectives. We should keep that in mind.

Shunning our brethren doesn't help us ascend hellish realms very easily or quickly. We have all forgotten our divinity and we are all here to learn and remember it.

Perspectives

She said, "There have been many times when
I've tried to shine light on the trap of hatred
only to be shunned by 'friends' who want to
make me the enemy. I am no one's enemy."

Perspectives

We can be aware of corruption and work to
make things better.

Anger might be a powerful catalyst. But what
toxic venom is hatred to the energy of any
human?

Many people don't seem to be aware of what
it eventually does to the physical being.

Choose wisely what vibration you allow to
linger in your sacred space.

Perspectives

About the Author

Janine Palmer (Spirit Silver Moon) grew up in Northern California and resides in Southern California today.

After devastating county-wide wildfires in Southern California and global economic collapse, Janine and her family endured physical, economical and emotional losses, along with the loss of friendships.

Judgmental treatment by so-called religious people (family/friends) caused her to question religions due to poor treatment by others in religious ideology.

These initiations tested her inner strength and caused her to investigate more deeply for truth, what brings true happiness, forward movement, the evolvement of the soul and ultimately, she discovered her calling.

She was a phoenix who rose from her own ashes with a powerful story to share of truth, strength, wisdom, compassion, love and taking one's power back. We must remember our magnificence to in order to rise above so much illusion.

Looking for answers, Janine Palmer (Silver Moon) extensively studied and continues to study multiple healing modalities for emotional and spiritual healing.

Janine has studied World Religions, Spirituality, Early Christianity, Gnosticism, Philosophy, Critical Thinking, Biblical Scholars, and Spiritual teachers. Janine is a Clinical Hypnotherapist and Shamanic Practitioner.

In the spiritual and emotional arenas, Janine has studied and become certified in the following areas: Cognitive Behavioral Hypnotherapy, Ericksonian Hypnosis, Energy Psychology, Emotional Freedom Technique (EFT or Tapping), Kinesiology, Muscle Testing, Neuro-linguistic Programming (NLP) the language of the mind, Reiki Master and Gamma Healing for overcoming energy vampires, healing emotional traumas, anxiety, depression and PTSD, and Shamanic Journey Work.

These modalities are helpful for releasing stress, old pain, resentment, anger, doubt, grief, unforgiveness or anything which blocks forward movement.

This knowledge and wisdom is contained within her writings of uplifting messages for healing.
She shares tools we can use to assist ourselves and others on their path.

Janine is the author of multiple books containing many genres and messages from various teachings and modalities. The four main genres are story poems, romance, rising above dogma and emotional and spiritual healing. These are presented as poetic tales which have received very positive support and feedback around the world.

Janine's compassion and calling to help others break free of limiting and painful situations can be felt through the writings contained her book series Divine Heretic. She does God's work for humanity, for the collective, and greater good. It is a gift and a blessing she is very grateful for.